CHRISTMAS IN THE
FOUR GOSPEL HOMES

CHRISTMAS IN THE FOUR GOSPEL HOMES

An Advent Study

Cynthia M. Campbell

WJK WESTMINSTER
JOHN KNOX PRESS
LOUISVILLE · KENTUCKY

Portions of this book were previously published as a downloadable study titled
"Christmas Accounts in the Gospels: An Adult Advent Study,"
The Thoughtful Christian, 2017, www.TheThoughtfulChristian.com.

First edition
Published by Westminster John Knox Press
Louisville, Kentucky

19 20 21 22 23 24 25 26 27 28—10 9 8 7 6 5 4 3 2 1

Book design by Erika Lundbom-Krift
Cover design by Mary Ann Smith

Library of Congress Cataloging-in-Publication Data

Names: Campbell, Cynthia McCall, author.
Title: Christmas in the four Gospel homes : an Advent study / Cynthia M.
  Campbell.
Description: Louisville, KY : Westminster John Knox Press, [2019] |
  Identifiers: LCCN 2019018113 (print) | LCCN 2019021848 (ebook) | ISBN
  9781611649680 (ebk.) | ISBN 9780664264994 (pbk. : alk. paper)
Subjects: LCSH: Jesus Christ--Nativity.--Biblical teaching. |
  Christmas--Biblical teaching. | Infancy narratives (Gospels)
Classification: LCC BT315.3 (ebook) | LCC BT315.3 .C36 2019 (print) | DDC
  242/.33--dc23
LC record available at https://lccn.loc.gov/2019018113

Most Westminster John Knox Press books are available at special quantity discounts when purchased in bulk by corporations, organizations, and special-interest groups. For more information, please e-mail SpecialSales@wjkbooks.com.

To the congregation of Highland Presbyterian Church
for their love, support, and partnership in ministry

CONTENTS

INTRODUCTION

ONCE AGAIN, WE ARE PUTTING UP THE DECORATIONS; we are singing carols and buying gifts. Once again, it is Advent. In these days between Thanksgiving and New Year's, many of us visit other people's homes. We may drop in for coffee or be invited to an open house. Some spend several days with relatives who live out of town. When we do this, it is always so interesting to see other people's homes—how they decorate, what kinds of things they cherish, how their styles mesh with their personalities. Tom Long, distinguished professor of preaching, has compared the church's lectionary (the three-year cycle of Sunday readings) to homes that the church goes to visit. The first year, the Gospel readings take us to Matthew's house; then we move on to Mark; finally, we visit Luke. Every year, on special occasions (notably in the season of Easter and some other special days) we go to visit John. Just like our own homes, each gospel house is quite different—decor and ambience reflect the family that lives there and their individual traditions. Some are cluttered; others are spare. Some are decorated within an inch of their lives; others are haphazard. We each like some more than others, but moving around allows us to savor the same things from different perspectives.

Some years ago, Jon Walton, then pastor of The First Presbyterian Church in the City of New York, used this idea as the basis for a sermon series during Advent. Building on his idea, I invite you on a journey to visit our four Gospel homes. The purpose of our journey is to experience what Christmas means from that perspective and how Christmas is celebrated there. Each chapter of this book is accompanied by a drawing of a house, the design of which is suggested by the shape and character of the Gospel. These drawings originally appeared on the cover of the Sunday bulletin when these chapters were preached as sermons. They are the creation of Kevin Burns, who has written his own interpretations of the Gospel home that welcomes us. Burns is an architect by profession and a deeply knowledgeable Bible teacher. I am deeply grateful to Kevin for making these theological reflections find visual expression. We hope that pondering each of the illustrations will draw you more deeply into this journey as we reflect on the mystery of Jesus, Son of God, born of Mary.

This book is for individual or group study. It includes prayers and questions for reflection for each chapter near the end of the book. Readers can respond in writing in the space given.

Finally, the book concludes with suggestions for leading a group study. I am grateful to Martha Bettis Gee for providing the original version of this guide and to David Maxwell for his valuable contributions in editing this material.

CHRISTMAS AT MARK'S HOUSE

Mark 1:1–11

WE BEGIN BY GOING TO VISIT COUSIN MARK. He lives in a spare, simple home, because Mark is kind of like the police detective who says, "Just the facts, ma'am." His house has just what it needs and not much more: a door, a couple of widows, a chimney. The surprising thing is that there isn't much in the way of Christmas going on here. There are no decorations to speak of, not a lot that makes us think of holiday cheer. As far as we know, Mark is the first of these writings that we call "Gospels," and we call them that largely because of how Mark starts: "The beginning of the good news [that is, the "gospel"] of Jesus Christ, the Son of God." It's an odd way to start, don't you think? I mean, why would you announce the beginning of something that the reader knows is the beginning? It would be like starting a sermon by saying, "Now I am starting my sermon for Advent, week one." Well, obviously.

Perhaps Mark means something else by "beginning." Where does the Gospel begin? How does this whole thing get launched? According to Mark, it starts with John the Baptist. In the ancient world, the arrival of the monarch required a herald. The herald (or messenger) was the press release or the Facebook post or the tweet of the ancient world. Back then, a guy was sent into the city to say, "Heads up—monarch sighting! Sweep the streets and clean up your act!" The good news begins with the messenger, and the message is, "Prepare the way of the Lord, make his paths straight." Out in the wilderness, at the edge of civilization, in a sort-of-scary liminal space, John is calling out for people to repent, to change their hearts and lives.

Baptism was the sign John offered people to signify their desire to prepare for the new thing John believed God was doing. Washed in the water of the River Jordan, the people were ready to start their lives with God anew. Some scholars suggest that this act of going through this water was to remind people of how God led their ancestors out of slavery and into freedom by passing through the water of the Red Sea. Among those who came to John was Jesus from Nazareth. When he came up from the water, Mark says, he saw the heavens torn open and the Spirit of God coming down like a dove. And he heard a voice saying to him, "You are my Beloved, my Son, my Child." Then that same Spirit drove Jesus deeper into the wilderness, where he fasted and prayed for forty days. His faith, his understanding of God, and his very identity were tested. When he returned to Galilee, he began to say, "The reign of God has come near." Jesus called a few followers and began a ministry of teaching and healing. By the end of chapter 1, Jesus is surrounded by crowds eager to hear his message. They are anxious, as well, for healing. For Mark, Jesus' acts of healing aren't just miracles; they are demonstrations of power. They point to the end of this Gospel and the truly good news that God is more powerful than suffering and death.

NO CHRISTMAS STORY?

That's it. That's Mark's beginning. In a very few quick brushstrokes, the saga of the good news is launched. Why no Christmas story? Why no hint even of Jesus' beginnings? All we know is that he came from Nazareth. A pretty slim résumé and not very enlightening. Some think that Mark doesn't include a story about Jesus' birth because he doesn't know one. Mark is writing about thirty years after Jesus' death and resurrection. Tradition says that, by this time, Peter and Paul have already been put to death in Rome. Other eyewitnesses are surely dying off. Mark wants to capture the story as it is being told in small communities of believers around the Mediterranean. He is the first one to commit this story to writing. Maybe he just doesn't know the part about Jesus' birth.

Frankly, I doubt that. I think Mark is both a skillful writer and an editor. Some think that Mark may have been a companion or protégé of Paul's. As we know, Paul is famously uninterested in the details of Jesus' life and ministry. "I preach Christ and him crucified," Paul wrote. Perhaps it is this theology, focused on the scandal of Christ's crucifixion and the triumph of resurrection, that shapes Mark's writing. Some have even called Mark's Gospel "a passion narrative with a long introduction." Indeed, this Gospel is structured around Jesus' predictions of his death and builds steadily to its dramatic conclusion. Christmas stories are left on the cutting room floor because they don't serve Mark's purposes. Mark knows (and tells us in his opening words) that Jesus is the Son of God. He doesn't need stories of a miraculous or mysterious birth to "prove" that. Jesus is the power of life over death. Birth stories are simply a distraction.

Mark may have been the first to think that Christmas was a distraction, but he was certainly not the last Christian to think so. Long before

Christmas became a festival of selling and buying, groups of Christians were skeptical about Christmas excess. Did you know that Christmas carols didn't appear in some Protestant hymnals until the late nineteenth and early twentieth centuries in the United States? There was a lot of Christmas celebration in colonial Williamsburg but not much in Puritan New England. Why? Because those followers of John Calvin believed that Sunday was the most important day and that Sunday observance should not be cluttered with other saints or festivals, including Christmas! Like Mark, those Christians held that the core of the Gospel was Jesus' death and resurrection. Therefore Sunday, the Lord's Day, should celebrate that alone. Anything else would be a distraction.

Don't panic. I know that many of you just got all the Christmas decorations out, and I'm not going to argue that we should put them back! I am proud to be a Reformed Christian, but there are things that well-meaning Reformers got wrong, and getting rid of Christmas was one of them. Reformed tradition is not wrong about what is at the heart of the good news: The good news of the gospel is not only the birth of a child. The good news is that the man who was the Son of God laid down his life for his friends and that God raised him from the dead as a sign that God's love conquers death.

FINDING HOPE

The Christmas season is well under way. Cherished traditions are surely appearing in your church, such as Advent wreaths, carol singing, special giving projects. There may be an upcoming children's Christmas pageant and Christmas Eve services to look forward to. But as the days grow shorter and light diminishes, many of us are anxious. So many things in our world seem unsettled and unknown. The nation seems to be deeply divided on major political issues. Many feel overlooked or sidelined. Racial injustice, particularly as that relates to poverty, unequal education, and incarceration, is once again in the news. Anti-immigrant sentiments have become common. Hateful and divisive rhetoric has taken the place of honest debate. Many are anxious, and the times seem out of joint.

Chirpy songs about Santa Clause won't get us very far in the face of the troubles we confront. Shopping, fun as it is, doesn't keep anxiety at bay for long. Old-time Christmas nostalgia doesn't insulate us from a broken and fearful world. Hope is what we need, but as Cousin Mark reminds us, hope is to be found in the manger only because it is found first on the cross. The hope that Mark offers is not in spite of suffering; it is hope that has been through suffering and emerged on the other side. From the very beginning of this fast-paced Gospel story, we know that Jesus is headed toward his death. Three times he attempts to prepare his disciples; three times they fail to understand; three times he explains (patiently) that following him means following the way of the cross. It seems utterly counterintuitive, but this is God's way. As Leonard Cohen wrote: "There's a crack in everything / That's how the light gets in."[1]

As a child, my family decorated for Christmas on the day after Thanksgiving. We didn't shop; we unwrapped boxes of Christmas decorations. Then on New Year's Day, after the Rose Parade was over, we put it all away. That's one of the problems with Christmas: we have a tendency to

1. Leonard Cohen, "Anthem," *The Future*, Columbia, 1992, compact disc.

think Christmas is something we get out once a year and then put away. We think of the Christmas season as something that has a beginning and an end. We celebrate the "holidays," and then we go back to business as usual, largely unchanged except maybe for the weight we've gained. But that's not the gospel. It's not a moment in time to be celebrated and then largely forgotten. The good news is about transformation. Jesus told us that the kingdom of God is at hand. He came to change your life forever. He came to bring you hope for your despair, and peace for your anxiety, and love so that you can stare down death.

Some of those really old Christmas carols got it right. One dates back to medieval times and was sung in Latin until it was translated in the mid-nineteenth century. "Good Christian friends, rejoice with heart and soul and voice; now ye need not fear the grave: Jesus Christ was born to save! / Calls you one and calls you all to gain the everlasting hall. / Christ was born to save! Christ was born to save!"[2]

---

2. John Mason Neale, "Good Christian Men, Rejoice," *Glory to God* (Louisville, KY: Westminster John Knox Press, 2013), 132.

CHRISTMAS AT MATTHEW'S HOUSE

Matthew 1:18–25; 2:13–15, 19–23

THERE ARE SOME HOMES WHERE EVERYWHERE YOU look there are family photos: in bookcases, on tables, even on top of the piano. Or perhaps there is a long stairway leading up from the entryway to the second floor, and all the way up, as far as the eye can see, there are pictures of family members, some smiling, some sad, and some faces that carry the marks of life's struggles. The clothing gets more and more dated the farther up you look. Perhaps the quality of the photographs changes; some colors fade with time. But there they are: a steady march of faces through time receding up the staircase. Pictures of extended family in our homes are some of our most precious possessions because they link today with yesterday, and as we teach younger family members the names that go with the faces, we lay a foundation for years to come.

This Advent season, we are imagining each Gospel as a home we visit for Christmas. Today, we come to Matthew. The house that Kevin Burns and I have imagined is a big, rambling Victorian. It is both welcoming and a little scary. This is a house with a past. If walls could talk, these would have stories to tell! Several generations have occupied this house in the past, and multiple generations live here today. There are photos and even a few portraits on all the walls. In this house, every Christmas ornament has a story—who bought them or made them, where and when, and who that person was and how (in a rather convoluted way) they are related to you. There is a party in full swing at Uncle Matthew's house; lot's of folks are there, but frankly, a few of them are a little strange. You get the feeling that they're not from around here and that they don't quite belong. But I'm getting ahead of myself.

JESUS' BEGINNINGS

The beginning of the Gospel of Matthew starts: "An account of the birth [literally the "genesis"] of Jesus the Messiah, the son of David, the son of Abraham. Abraham was the father of Isaac, and Isaac the father of Jacob, and Jacob the father of Judah and his brothers . . ."—all the way to King David. Then the names continue down to the exile in Babylon, and after the exile to Joseph, the husband of Mary.

Right away, we can tell that there is something a bit odd about this. This is not exactly an Ancestry.com list. It is theologically driven, not data driven. In the first place, Matthew makes everything neat: fourteen generations. In the Hebrew way of thinking, seven was the perfect number (think days of creation plus the day God rested). This ordering of generations is thus "perfection times two." In order to make this work, Matthew has taken a few liberties with the listing of kings found elsewhere in the Old Testament. The truth Matthew has in mind is more symbolic than it is literal.

Second, we would expect such a recounting of generations to stick to the "great men" of the past. Indeed, that's how it begins: Abraham, the father of Isaac; Isaac, the father of Jacob; Jacob, the father of Judah. But then the patriarchal list is interrupted. First, there is Tamar, the daughter-in-law of Judah, whom Judah takes to be a prostitute but who eventually gives birth to two of his sons (see Genesis 38). Then there is Rahab the prostitute, who hid the Israelite spies as they attempted to infiltrate Canaan. Then there is Ruth of Moab (Israel's neighbor and sometime enemy), who pledges covenant loyalty to her mother-in-law, Naomi; immigrates with Naomi back to Bethlehem; and eventually becomes the grandmother of David (see the book of Ruth). Bathsheba is not mentioned by name, but she is there too. Her first son (born after the murder of her husband, Uriah) died, but her second son was David's greatest heir, Solomon (see 2

Samuel 11 and 12). All these amazing women play key roles in Israel's story and thus in the story of Jesus. Embedded in their stories are important virtues. These women demand justice. They are courageous and loyal, and without them, the story does not go forward.

On these journeys to the homes of the four Gospels, we are asking: Where does each author think that the good news begins? Mark begins with John the Baptist, the herald or messenger who announces the arrival of Jesus, God's Messiah. For Matthew, the beginning (the genesis) of the good news is Abraham. Where does Jesus come from? Matthew's answer is from ancient Israel. He is a child of Abraham, born to the covenant God made long ago. Jesus is also descended from King David, son of Jesse. Israel had been waiting for centuries for a new king, a good, just, and upright leader who would restore the nation and help the people return to God. Jesus is the "son of the covenant" and the "son of David." He is also the descendant of all those strong and faithful women. Jesus is the heir of what God has been doing all these centuries. You can see the family resemblance in all the pictures hanging around the house.

But there's more here than a genealogy. As Matthew tells the story of Jesus' birth, he wants us, his audience, to remember many other parts of the biblical story. First of all, there is Joseph, the espoused husband of Mary. He was a dreamer. Four times in this story, he is visited by an angel, a messenger of God. The angel tells him that Mary's unexpected child is God's own doing. Joseph is to name him "Jesus," which means "God saves," because that is Jesus' vocation and destiny. Then later, the angel warns Joseph to take mother and child and flee to Egypt to escape King Herod's murderous decree to kill any supposed pretenders to his throne. After some years in Egypt, Joseph is advised in a dream that it is safe to return to Israel. One last dream sends them farther out of harm's way, to Nazareth. Matthew's first audience, a largely Jewish Christian community, immediately thinks of another Joseph—one of the sons of Judah, the dreamer with the coat of many colors whose dreams made his brothers so angry that they sold him into slavery in Egypt. But once there, Joseph was able to interpret his dreams and the dreams of others and soon became an adviser to the pharaoh. He eventually used this ability to save the whole region from famine and to bring his family to safety in Egypt.

Matthew also wants his readers to remember Moses. When Israel was enslaved in Egypt, Pharaoh ordered all male infants born to Israelites to be put to death. Moses was rescued by his mother and sister; his life was preserved from a tyrant's rage, just like Jesus'. Later, of course, it was Moses who led his people out of Egypt from slavery to freedom; Jesus was brought home from Egypt to fulfill his destiny to lead humanity from death to life eternal.

In all of this, Matthew is pointing to all those pictures that line the walls and saying, "See, Jesus comes from us! He is one of us! Our story is his story! Jesus has more than a family resemblance to Israel. Our whole history is right there in his own young life." To drive the point home, five times in these first two chapters Matthew says that something happened "in order to fulfill what was spoken through the prophet." We may think that Matthew is just "proof-texting," that is, citing these ancient stories as a way to lend legitimacy to the story of Jesus. But Matthew's point is much subtler than that. He is not trying to prove a point as much as he is attempting to show the deep relationship between the story of Jesus and the story of Israel. He is embedding Jesus in the religious heritage of his audience.

And so who is Jesus? In the words of Isaiah, to whom Matthew appeals, he is "Immanuel"— literally, "with us God." The God who has been with us since Abraham; the God who spoke to Joseph the dreamer; the God who heard our cry in slavery and sent Moses to lead us to freedom; the God who has been with us all the way down that long line of photographs on the wall: that same God is with us here and now in Jesus, son of Abraham, son of David, son of Mary, Son of God. God has not forgotten us; with us is God.

OUTSIDERS?

So far, this is an inspiring family story. Through tragedy and triumph, disaster and delight, high moments and terrible loss: through it all, God has kept God's promises to the family of

Abraham. But then there are these other folks who have come to the big family party at Matthew's house. We know who they are, but what exactly are they doing here? In a big family where everyone is related to everyone else, some of these folks are pretty clearly "outsiders." So what do we make of them?

First of all, there are the women. The most striking thing about Matthew's list of Jesus' ancestors is that women are even mentioned. In a traditional, patriarchal culture, women are by definition "outsiders." But the truly surprising thing is that Matthew mentions these women in particular. At least two of them, and probably three, are not Israelites; they are not daughters of Abraham and Sarah. Rahab is a Canaanite; Ruth is from Moab; Bathsheba is the wife of Uriah the Hittite. From one way of looking at covenant history, we say that these women do not belong. They are not Israelites. But they nevertheless play a vital role in God's promise-keeping. Startling as their presence is, it is evidence of God's covenant promise to Abraham: through him, all the families of earth will be blessed. The good news of the gospel is the fulfillment of this promise that God's covenant love is for all humankind.

The other outsiders, of course, are the magi. This is the part of Matthew's Christmas story that we know best. From literally out of nowhere, "wise men from the east" appear in Jerusalem saying that they are following a star that is the sign of the birth of a king of the Jews. In the world of Jesus' day, it is likely they were from Persia (modern-day Iran). Despite the Christmas carol, these are not kings; they are astrologers. Like many others in the ancient world, they thought that the movement of the planets and stars could reveal the future. In a way, they were early scientists because of their careful observation of astronomical events. But theologically, their ideas had no place in the thought-world of Israel. God made the stars; they were God's creatures, just like human beings. Stars don't hold the key to the future, Israel says; the Creator does. But here are these magi, convinced that something they saw portended a great, new thing. They have not come as curiosity seekers but as worshipers. Their tradition is different, but their goal is to bring their offerings and to bow in wonder.

CONCLUSION

Christmas at Matthew's house is a huge gathering of extended family. But it is also a home where those who would otherwise be seen as outsiders are not only welcome but have pride of place. Their pictures are also on the wall. They belong here along with all the rest. When we say that Jesus is Immanuel—"God with us"—it turns out that "us" is not just the extended family or the ones who share a birthright. The "us" is *all of us*: the whole human family. And whenever we sing "for unto us a child is born, unto us a son is given," it's not the "little us"—the people just like us—it's the great, big "us."

This is what we learn at Matthew's house: God's promise is indeed for Israel, but (as God promised Abraham and Sarah) it is for so many, many more. God's vision encompasses both those to whom God has revealed Godself and the whole world and all who are made in God's image. God's promise is indeed for those of us who find our heart's true home in Jesus Christ. But it is also for the whole world that God loves so much. This is a day to sing, "Joy to the world, the Lord is come!"

CHRISTMAS AT LUKE'S HOUSE

Luke 2:1–14

THERE ARE MANY REASONS WHY HAVING A LIVE nativity display on the front lawn of the church is a bad idea. Cleanup is one of the obvious reasons. General liability is another. But the principal reason has to do with what happened to a church some years back. A big, well-to-do congregation in a North Dallas neighborhood decided to have a live nativity display for several nights close to Christmas: great publicity, a gift to the neighborhood, a gentle reminder that "Jesus is the reason for the season!" So they built a shed and recruited Mary and Joseph, shepherd and kings, and animals. Now anybody can bring in some sheep and a donkey, maybe even a goat. But because this happened in Texas, the lowing cattle were replaced with a Texas longhorn steer. Now I don't know that a longhorn steer is any more skittish or stubborn than any other kind of cow, but this one had a mind of its own. Somehow it managed to escape its tether not once but twice, and *Texas Monthly* magazine reported that it was the senior pastor who ran through the neighborhood chasing it down.

The reason we have nativity displays—live or otherwise—is because of St. Francis of Assisi. About eight hundred years ago, Francis was concerned that the feast of Christmas had become an occasion mostly for gifts and parties. He wanted Christians to remember that this was about the birth of Jesus, and so he created the now-famous tableau, like the one on display in the front of many sanctuaries today. The first nativity scenes were live and outdoors, of course, but over the centuries, artists fashioned the characters out of wood and clay. Some were very simple; others were elaborate, the characters dressed in fine clothing and jewels. Soon these displays figured prominently in churches all across Europe. For people who could not read the story, it was a way to make it come alive as a focus for devotion and prayer. And people have been making and collecting crèches ever since.

LUKE'S FULLY DECORATED HOUSE

In this chapter, we visit the third Gospel house on our journey through Advent. First, we went to Mark's spare and plain cottage. Then we visited Matthew's huge Victorian crammed with both relatives and strangers. Today, we visit Luke's house. As you can see, Kevin Burns has portrayed this house as an open and welcoming ranch house. Kids are playing in the yard, which they share with a variety of animals. There is a full porch that invites visitors to stop by for a visit. Everything about this house says, "welcome!" At Christmas time, Luke's place is decorated within an inch of its life. There are lights everywhere and Christmas trees in several rooms. Among the displays on the front lawn is a live nativity (complete with llama!). Christmas carols are playing from loudspeakers mounted on the roof. It is a joyous place and open to all.

Luke is the Gospel that gives us the Christmas we know best and love the most, with mother and child in the first wonderful moments of cherishing the miracle of birth. The setting is a place of warmth and safety, despite there being no room in the inn. Angels fill the night sky with wondrous music. Shepherds abide in the fields, keeping watch over their flocks by night—just like young David did before he was anointed by Samuel, later to become king. And young Mary ponders everything in her heart. Christmas at Luke's house is just what we all want most: beauty and joy and peace.

LUKE'S GOSPEL
BEFORE THE GOSPEL

But in fact, there is a good deal more going on at Luke's house than meets the eye. With each of our Gospel visits, we have been asking: Where does the good news begin? With Mark, it begins with John the Baptist, the herald or messenger who prepares the way for the Messiah. Matthew begins with Abraham, to whom God promised not only children in his old age but also a channel of blessing for the whole human family. Like Matthew, Luke has a "backstory" to Jesus' ministry. But Luke doesn't just tell us about the birth of Jesus. He spends an entire chapter (eighty verses!) on what came before that. It is, as one commentator writes, the "gospel before the gospel."[1]

Before looking closely at this intriguing prequel to Christmas, we need to notice that the first three chapters of Luke are like videos, each of which has a time/date stamp on it. Chapter 1 (after the brief introduction, v. 5) begins: "In the days of King Herod of Judea, there was a priest named Zechariah." Then chapter 2 starts: "In those days a decree went out from Emperor Augustus that all the world should be registered. This was the first registration and was

1. N. T. Wright, *Luke for Everyone* (Louisville, KY: Westminster John Knox Press, 2004), 14.

taken while Quirinius was governor of Syria."
Finally, chapter 3 (where Luke introduces John
the Baptist) begins: "In the fifteenth year of the
reign of Emperor Tiberius, when Pontius Pilate
was governor of Judea, and Herod [son of King
Herod] was ruler of Galilee . . ."

On the one hand, these are what they appear
to be: time/date stamps. Events in the ancient
world were often dated in relationship to reign-
ing monarchs. If you don't have an absolute
calendar, this is simply how you tell time. But
recently, biblical scholars have been suggesting
that Luke is doing more than orienting his readers in time. He is also locating them theologically and politically. N. T. Wright describes the
opening of chapter 2 like this:

> Augustus was the adopted son of Julius Cae-
> sar. He became sole ruler of the Roman world
> after a bloody civil war in which he overpow-
> ered all rival claimants. . . . [He] turned the
> great Roman republic into an empire, with
> himself at the head; he proclaimed that he
> had brought justice and peace to the whole
> world; and, declaring his dead adoptive father
> to be divine, styled himself as "son of god."
> . . . Augustus, people said, was the "savior" of

the world. He was its king, its "lord." Increasingly, in the eastern part of his empire, people worshiped him, too, as a god.[2]

Luke is writing long after Augustus was dead, but the empire continued, and worshiping the emperor was part of the fabric of all those towns and cities where the new Christian communities were being formed. Reverencing the emperor was just what you did at the beginning of the Rotary Club meetings in Corinth and Philippi and Athens. It was even stamped on the money: "Caesar Augustus—son of god." *That's* the setting in which the angels sing. The heavenly music that floats over a weary world is not just a pious sentiment. It is a statement about who is *really* God. "Fear not," said the angel. "For behold, I bring you good tidings of great joy, which shall be to all people. For unto you is born this day in the city of David [a backwater, nothing village to the Romans, but ground zero of Israel's greatest king] a Savior, who is Christ [the Messiah], the Lord." All those imperial

2. Wright, *Luke for Everyone*, 22–23.

titles, Luke tells us, *really* belong to this newborn child.

At Luke's house, we walk through all the beautiful and familiar scenes of Christmas—the crèche, the carols, the warm and peaceful glow. And then we are invited deeper into the house and deeper into the story. Here the good news doesn't begin with Jesus. It doesn't begin with John the Baptist. It begins with John the Baptist's parents. Zechariah and Elizabeth are old. No matter how good and fulfilling their lives and their marriage had been, they were without children. In the worldview of the time, it was Elizabeth's problem: she was barren. But being childless also meant that this couple had no future: there would be no one to care for them in old age, no one to mourn their deaths, no one to carry on their legacy and names. Then one day, as Zechariah was serving as priest in the Temple in Jerusalem, an angel appeared and told him that he and Elizabeth (at long last) would become parents. And it was the story of Abraham and Sarah all over again: when life seemed almost over, God gave the gift of new life. To those who had no hope, God gave the gift of the future.

Luke's crafting of this gospel before the gospel is both intricate and powerful. There are two appearances by the angel Gabriel: first to Zechariah and then to Mary. They are perfect contrasts: an old man and a young girl, a priest of the great Temple in Jerusalem and a peasant from a small town far from the city. He protests and asks the angel for a sign; she receives the angel's news with courageous grace. Zechariah is made speechless by the angel: nine months of silence so that he can really learn what is going on. Mary immediately sets out on a journey to be with her cousin Elizabeth, and then she sings the most amazing song.

LUKE'S THEMES

It is the songs of these two—Mary and Zechariah—that embody the good news. They are the overture to Luke's Gospel. Mary's song (Luke 1:46–55) is about what God is going to do in the world and to the world. Mary sings about the future in the past tense, because to the eyes of faith, God's victory has already happened, and it is radical stuff. God has brought down the powerful from their thrones and lifted up the lowly, filled the hungry with good things, and sent the rich away empty. The world has been turned upside down: power no longer belongs to the rich; food (which means life) is available to the hungry poor; those who already have enough aren't getting more.

Zechariah's song (Luke 1:68–79) carries the same themes: God will redeem God's people, save them from their enemies, and give them freedom to worship God without fear. Zechariah sings about his son John's ministry. John is the one who will prepare the way for the Messiah, whom Zechariah calls "Dayspring," the one who will bring light to those who sit in darkness and the shadow of death and who will guide people into the way of peace. These two songs have been so influential that they have been featured at the heart of Christian worship for centuries. The song of Zechariah (known by its Latin title the "Benedictus") is always sung or recited at morning prayer, while the song of Mary (or the "Magnificat") is sung or said at evening prayer.

Just as the overture to a ballet, opera, or musical announces the melodies that will be heard later, the songs of Mary and Zechariah set the tone for the entire Gospel of Luke. Jesus' ministry begins with a sermon in Nazareth, where he announces his mission to preach good news to the poor, release to captives, recovery of sight to the blind, and liberty to the oppressed. Jesus has more to say about money, poverty, and the care of the poor in this Gospel than in any other. Jesus proclaims the reign of God, and Luke makes it clear that God's reign is present in the words and actions of Jesus. His parables celebrate finding the lost and reuniting those who are estranged. Tax collectors and other sinners are welcome in Jesus' company. Women are part of the company of followers and are featured as friends of Jesus. Gentiles are featured prominently (for example, the Roman officer who asks Jesus to heal his slave and the parable of the Good Samaritan). Jesus has indeed come both to be a light to enlighten the Gentiles and to be the glory of God's people Israel (Luke 2:29–32).

For Mary, Zechariah, and Luke the Gospel writer, all of this is the sign that God has not forgotten God's people or the promises made long before. God remembers those promises, in particular the ones made to Abraham and Sarah: there will be a future, a future of blessing for the whole human family. Is that what was going on in the world where John and Jesus were born? No. Is that what Mary and Zechariah *saw* with their eyes? Was there evidence for any of this? No again. But at Luke's house, we see with the eyes of faith, and (God willing) we shape our lives accordingly. Once again, we have heard good news: that despite all the signs to the contrary, God has not forgotten us; God has not forgotten God's world; God has not abandoned God's most broken and needy people. The birth of Jesus is best proclaimed in the song of "angels bending near the earth" who proclaim peace to a broken world. And once again we are invited to "rest beside the weary road, and hear the angels sing."[3]

3. Edmund Hamilton Sears, "It Came Upon the Midnight Clear," *Glory to God* (Louisville, KY: Westminster John Knox Press, 2013), 123.

CHRISTMAS AT JOHN'S HOUSE

John 1:1–5, 14

IN THIS ADVENT JOURNEY, WE HAVE IMAGINED EACH of the four Gospels as a home we are visiting for Christmas. We've been to Mark's simple, spare cottage where the celebration of Christmas is so muted as to be almost absent. Then we went to Matthew's rambling Victorian, with its fascinating cast of characters and deep and complex past. Then we stopped by to visit with

Luke and savored the deep beauty of Christmas decorations, food, and song, along with the live nativity scene on the front lawn.

As we have made our Advent journey to Christmas, we have asked: Where does each Gospel writer think that the good news of Jesus Christ begins? How does this author choose to start the story? For Mark, Matthew, and Luke, the good news begins at some point in human history: With John the Baptist, says Mark. With John's father, Zechariah, and the angel's announcement of John's birth, says Luke. For Matthew, it goes all the way back to God's promise to Abraham. But John takes us someplace else entirely. Most commentators today think that John knew the other three Gospels but wanted to retell the story of Jesus from his own, distinctive point of view. And John's house is like no other!

After John Glenn became the first American to orbit Earth in 1962, human beings could see our planet as a whole for the first time. We could actually see Earth brightly illuminated against the blackness of space. Perhaps the most famous photograph from space was the spectacular "blue marble" image of Earth produced by NASA in 2002. It's what we might call a "God's eye view" of Earth—our tiny, fragile, spectacularly beautiful home. There is a reproduction of this image—Earth hanging almost like a Christmas ornament against a deep, black sky—on the wall at John's house.

The first problem in visiting John's house is finding the house itself. The directions are a little sketchy. The house, you see, is set far off the main road. Once you find the driveway, you wind down a long, dark road, trees pressing in on both sides. Just when you think you're completely lost, you round a curve, go up a hill, and there it is—a fabulous home that looks as if it is made out of light, a light that shines in the deep darkness.

IN THE BEGINNING

Nowhere is John's uniqueness more obvious than in the beginning. "In the beginning"—*en arche* (in Greek). The first words of John's Gospel are the same as the opening words of Genesis, translated into Greek, which is the way first-century Jews knew the Hebrew Bible. "In the beginning"—this repetition is not an accident. This, John says, is where the good news of Jesus Christ really starts—at the beginning of everything. Just as Genesis does, John transports us back through time and space to the moment when time and space began, to the instant just before the Big Bang, when all there was, was God. And that, says John, is where it all started. The moment of creation is also the beginning of the story of redemption. The story of the beginning of life carries within it the promise that life is stronger than death.

These opening lines of the Gospel of John are the first things that most people learn when they begin to study Greek. The vocabulary is very simple: *God, word, life, darkness, light.* But these ordinary words are stuffed with extraordinary meaning. What was in the beginning with God, John says, was "the Word." According to Genesis, creation happened when God spoke. The "big bang," in other words, was an utterance, a speech-act, a word. Just as God spoke creation into being, so also God spoke the law to Moses. Later on, prophets delivered "the word of the Lord" to God's people. Later still, the author of the book of Proverbs celebrated an extension of this idea, one called "Lady Wisdom" who was present with God at creation: "When [God] established the heavens, I was there . . . I was daily [God's] delight . . . rejoicing in [God's] inhabited world and delighting in the human race" (Prov. 8:27–31). At the beginning, Wisdom/Word was embedded in creation. In other words, God made the world to be understood and cherished.

GOD IS ONE OF US

According to Genesis, God's first words were, "Let there be light!" According to John, what came into being through the Word was light that shines in the darkness. And the darkness will never "grasp" the light. There is a double meaning here: darkness will never apprehend the light, but it will also never comprehend it either. Darkness will never extinguish God's light because it will never truly understand it. Then John takes a step beyond Genesis: the Word became flesh and lived among us. That is to say, God has come among us as one of us. By this we know for certain that God is not far off in some distant heaven or so far back in the dim reaches of time that God doesn't matter. God is not the master clockmaker who set the universe running like a massive machine but has gone off to let everything run on its own. No, God has come among us to know us from the inside out. The Word became flesh and "lived among us," John says. The phrase literally means to "pitch a tent." We might say, "God moved into the neighborhood." And nothing about us—joy or sorrow, good or evil, brokenness or triumph—none of that is alien to God.

Irenaeus said that God became what we are in order to make us what God is.[1] This is amazingly good news. The point of the incarnation is our transformation. The Word became us—flesh and blood—so that we might become what we were *meant* to be. Remember how Genesis said we human beings were made? It was in the "image and likeness of God." Our true identity is to be reflections of the divine. We are the

---

1. Irenaeus, *Against Heresies*, book V., preface, in *Ante-Nicene Fathers,* http://gnosis.org/library/advh5.htm.

creatures meant to be most truly like God, who is the source of all that is good and beautiful and true.

Of course, we have messed this up royally. Our history as a human family is brutal and sordid. We go to war with each other, tolerate poverty and oppression, and fail to protect the earth, our home. Each of us carries the scars of things done to us and the unhealed memories of wrongs we have done. We carry anger and shame. Saddest of all, we carry resignation: That's just the way it is, we say. There's nothing we can really do to change it, we say. But that is precisely the idea that the incarnation is meant to dispel once and for all. God became what we are in order to make us what God is: that is, in order to set us free from all that hurt and brokenness and shame. The Word was made flesh so that we can be restored as the beautiful and loving people we are meant to be.

THE POWER OF LIFE

Light is one powerful metaphor in John's Gospel. The other is life. The life of the Word is the light that shines in the darkness. In John's Gospel, Jesus teaches us to see that life is more than being alive. Jesus has come to lead us to eternal or abundant life. In order to find this life, we must be born *anothen*—a Greek word that means both "again" and "from above," that is, from God. We are born "from above" when we believe or trust in the One who is from above. This is what Jesus tells Nicodemus. To the seeker, Jesus gives "living water," that is, water that brings eternal life. This is what Jesus tells the woman at the well. In his discourse or teaching that follows the miracle of the loaves and fishes, Jesus says, "I am the living bread that came down from heaven. Whoever eats of this bread will live forever; and the bread that I will give for the life of the world is my flesh" (6:51). Finally, as he prepares his disciples for his death, Jesus says that he is the vine and we are his branches. If we stay connected to the vine (if we "abide" in him), we will live, and our lives will bear rich and abundant fruit. All of this is the result of God's desire to restore what has been ruptured, to mend what has been broken, and to bring back those who have wandered off.

REDEMPTION AND HOPE

This is why we like stories about second chances. This is why we go to movies about flawed people who struggle against seemingly insurmountable odds and find the strength to prevail. In so many ways, these are Gospel stories, stories of redemption and hope. What the Gospel reminds us is that this longing for a second chance and the energy to struggle comes from deep down inside us, where God resides. And in our struggle, we are not alone, because the Word that was with God at creation is among us—right here, right now.

John's house may be hard to find, but once we are there, we learn the most beautiful and powerful truth of all: the light shines in the darkness, and darkness will not—because it cannot—overcome the light.

ONE LAST STOP

A POPULAR NONRELIGIOUS CHRISTMAS SONG BEGINS, "Over the river and through the woods, to grandmother's house we go." It conjures up a time of horses and sleighs and winter wonderlands. Not many of us have exactly this experience, but many visit grandparents and extended family for Christmas. Whether you live with or visit those generations older than your parents, what you experience is tradition. You learn about the values that shape your family. You come to understand where you come from. These pasts of ours shape us, and if we are fortunate, they shape us for the good.

In this Advent season, we have imagined each of the four Gospels as a home that we have visited. We have been with Mark, Matthew, Luke, and John to experience how Christmas— the coming of Jesus, the Messiah, the Son of God—is celebrated in each place. But there is one more house to visit. Just like us, the Gospel writers had spiritual grandparents. In fact, all the Gospels share one relative in common: the great prophet Isaiah. Biblical scholars tell us that what we know as the book of Isaiah represents the life and times of at least three different prophets. One, the "First Isaiah" (chapters 1–39), lived in Jerusalem before the nation of Judah was defeated and the city of Jerusalem was destroyed in 585 BCE. The "Second Isaiah" (chapters 40–60) wrote decades later to those who had been captured and were living in exile in Babylon. "Third Isaiah" was written still later as new generations were returning to the devastated city of Jerusalem and beginning the backbreaking work of rebuilding not only the city but also their national and religious identity. As centuries passed, the work of these three became one, largely because of the clear and coherent vision of God's promise of redemption, not only for Israel, but for the entire human community. It is almost impossible to imagine the story of Jesus without these visionaries who lived more than five hundred years before Jesus' birth but whose words and faith and hope shaped Jesus and his followers and, two thousand years later, us. The early church called Isaiah the "fifth Gospel" and used its words to tell the story of Jesus.

The question the Gospel writers sought to answer was: Who is Jesus? Matthew finds this answer in Isaiah: He is a child called "Immanuel"—"God with us" (Isa. 7:14). He is God in our midst, God on our side, and God for us. He is the Messiah, God's chosen and anointed one who inherits all the titles of honor and majesty: "Wonderful Counselor, Mighty God, Everlasting Father, Prince of Peace" (Isa. 9:6). He is the descendant of David, Israel's greatest king, and God's spirit will rest on him, the spirit of wisdom and understanding. In his world, he will judge the poor with honesty and integrity and stand by the poor of the earth. Under his rule, the wolf and the lamb will live together, and there will be peace in creation as well as among people (Isa. 11:1–9).

The Gospel writers found much more in the scroll of Isaiah. The ministry of John the Baptist seemed to be perfectly described in Isaiah 40:3–5:

> A voice cries out: "In the wilderness prepare the way of the LORD. . . . Every valley shall be lifted up, and every mountain and hill be made low . . . the glory of the LORD shall be revealed, and all people shall see it together!"

Just as Isaiah called people to turn to God in trust and with lives of renewed integrity, so John embodied that call as he prepared the way for Jesus.

Later, when Luke writes about the beginning of Jesus' ministry, he describes him in the synagogue reading from Isaiah:

> The spirit of the Lord GOD is upon me, because the LORD . . . has sent me to bring

> good news to the oppressed, to bind up the
> brokenhearted, to proclaim liberty to the cap-
> tives, and release to the prisoners; to proclaim
> the year of the LORD's favor. (Isa. 61:1–2)

And that's what they saw in Jesus' ministry: welcome for the outcast, forgiveness for the sinner, healing for the broken in body and in spirit, hope for the downtrodden, good news for the poor, and embrace of the stranger.

And when it came time for the Gospel writers and early Christian preachers to explain why Jesus, God's chosen one, had to suffer and die, they turned back to Isaiah and found this: "Surely he has borne our infirmities and carried our diseases . . . he was wounded for our transgressions, crushed for our iniquities" (Isa. 53:4–5). The suffering and death of God's anointed was not what anyone expected. The Messiah was supposed to be the one who had the power to defeat Israel's enemies. Jesus' shameful death by crucifixion was surely proof that he was not God's anointed. And yet, here are Isaiah's words about the Suffering Servant, whose suffering was the sign of God's compassion and the power of redeeming love.

Finally, as we look to the transformations ushered in by Jesus' resurrection, we use Isaiah's words again:

> For I am about to create new heavens and a new earth [God says]. . . . I am about to create Jerusalem as a joy, and its people as a delight. . . . No more shall there be in it an infant that lives but a few days, or an old person who does not live out a lifetime. . . . They shall build houses and inhabit them; they shall plant vineyards and eat their fruit. . . . They shall not labor in vain, or bear children for calamity. . . . Before they call I will answer, while they are yet speaking I will hear." (Isa. 65:17–25)

Those who first shared Christian faith, those whose preaching shaped the Christian movement, needed resources from their faith tradition. Where would they turn? They drew on the stories of Moses, Elijah, and Elisha. References to the Psalms abound in the Gospels and in Paul. But no influence is as powerful as Isaiah, an ancient treasure that seemed to have just the right words and images to express what Jesus was and is.

If we are fortunate, we have family, teachers,

and mentors who pass on to us gifts of wisdom from the past. Their words can give us courage and hope, visions that become the wellspring of our values and the source of our commitment to build a better world for our children and for all people. Each year, when we remember Jesus' birth, the coming of God's Messiah, may we hold in our hearts the hope we learn from our ancestor Isaiah. And may that hope shape our lives in the year to come. Amen.

Artist's Reflections

BY KEVIN BURNS

ARTIST'S REFLECTIONS
ON MARK'S HOUSE

I STARTED WITH MARK'S HOUSE. MARK IS UNDERstood to be the first Gospel written, and it provides much of the narrative spine for the other Synoptic Gospels. Thus it lacks some of the embellishment that the later Gospel writers would add to reinforce their own literary perspectives. Its first words explain its purpose: a presentation of the good news of Jesus, the mysterious suffering messiah we know to be Jesus. His identity as the suffering savior is fundamental to understanding who he is and what he is about. Even as the author presents this identity in a straightforward manner for the reader, few characters in the story (other than God, Jesus, and the demons) recognize this reality.

Unlike other Gospels, Mark does not include detailed theological expositions on how this Messiah is the answer to what Judaism needs. Mark simply presents a good story, told with the excitement of a modern storyteller rushing from scene to scene. It lacks the refined syntax expected by the hellenized first-century world of Greek-speaking intellectuals. Mark is spare on detail. The opening chapters skip past any suggestion of a quaint birth story. The author omits anything unnecessary to the story or superfluous to the author's point. Yet there is clarity in presenting Jesus as a unique man who is empowered with authority from above to teach, heal, and affect change in the human beings he meets. He does not seek glorious acknowledgments. He encourages those who witness his miracles to keep quiet about them. And while this may make his works seem understated, he shines with an unvarnished, idealized humanity that repeatedly demonstrates that, in the end, love will overcome, no matter what the worldly powers do to crush him. There is an admirable simplicity to this portrayal of Jesus.

In thinking about the nature of this Gospel, I found myself pondering the fundamental essentials of the concept of "house." To be consistent with Mark's Gospel, only the essentials should be included (roof, entrance, window, etc.). I was drawn to images of the most basic dwellings seen across the rural landscapes that are ubiquitous to many agrarian societies in many countries. The sketched house is a manifestation of the most basic and fundamental elements of a simple residential structure. There is a single door in the center framed by two windows. The roof form is a simple gable. Material is unadorned, with no pretense. However, it might be said that this simplicity of form expresses the idea of house while simultaneously capturing the emotive and cultural complexity of what is meant by the word *home*. Mark's Gospel is much the same in how it portrays the fundamental nature of Christ. The reader doesn't need long monologues or dense symbolic sermons on the nature of light and darkness. The compelling narrative highlights an admirable character revealing to his world the true nature of God.

ARTIST'S REFLECTIONS
ON MATTHEW'S HOUSE

THE GOSPEL OF MATTHEW SHARES MUCH OF ITS content with Mark. But the differences are notable. Matthew presents a Jesus that sees himself as the fulfillment of Judaism. Matthew is a Gospel that seeks to connect Jesus to this sacred Jewish history, even presenting Jesus as a second Moses who, as a child, barely escapes death at the hands of a jealous monarch. Jesus celebrates a glorious crossing through the great waters of baptism instead of the Red Sea, and he climbs up his own version of a mountain to provide instruction to the people about the truth of God's Torah. In the Sermon on the Mount, Jesus even reinterprets the contemporary understanding of the law in a way that Matthew describes as fulfilling the law. From the beginning, the writer of the Gospel of Matthew emphasizes that Jesus is from a long ancestry of important Jewish figures, such as Abraham and King David (and other famous people in the genealogy, some with more sordid histories). There is an allusion to mystery and intrigue. The birth story is full of violence and people fleeing toward safety. There are mysterious strangers from distant unknown places. These are stories of intrigue and intensity, but they are also stories that need to be told and that need to be heard.

The Matthew house needed to be traditional, with recognizable residential details and components, but it also needed to be mysterious, inviting us to explore the mystery with a healthy amount of trepidation. We approach with care, and the skin tingles a little as we go inside. Most people have childhood memories of a house in their neighborhood or town that was beautiful but a little scary. I was drawn to the image of a gothic-revival house that I remember walking by when I was younger. Just looking at it from the outside, one knew there could be secret rooms and forgotten memories deep inside the building. One wanted to go inside, but only in the light of the day, and only with someone who helped you to feel safe. This image evokes the kind of house one imagines when reading a scary story. It is the kind of place seen in nightmares and scary movies.

While the house's appearance communicates mystery and danger, it also suggests a rich history that invites us to come inside and hear the stories of long-gone ancestors. It is impossible to view this house from the outside and be certain as to the number of rooms that may be inside, each with its own walls that we may wish could speak to us, sharing the rich stories they have witnessed during the life and history of the house's existence.

As adults, we know that we can learn from hard stories. We know that we all have skeletons in our closets, and we all have some history that might be a source of shame rather than pride. But as we age, we learn to accept these truths of our past and recognize that even the uncomfortable stories shape who we are. The Bible does not avoid the flaws of its main characters. Instead, it weaves a rich tapestry of stories that showcase some of humanity's scariest aptitudes throughout history. But like the winding corridors that connect the internal rooms of this gothic-revival house, the diverse stories in our biblical tradition are connected by an overarching story that emphasizes that God's fundamental concern is love and human redemption.

ARTIST'S REFLECTIONS
ON LUKE'S HOUSE

LUKE IS THE GOSPEL WITH THE MOST IMAGERY THAT we think of at Christmastime as we decorate our own homes for the season. This is the text with the host of angels heralding the glory of God. In this Gospel, the humble shepherds in the fields are visited by the angelic messengers and are invited to go to Bethlehem to see the Christ child. Mary and Joseph end up in rustic lodging, due to the mass of people visiting the city, and the beautiful and humble birth scene is transformed into the inspiration for a multitude of manger scenes that have become common decoration for homes all around the world.

The Gospel according to Luke is packed with details and stories that find middle ground between the rushed pace of Mark's narrative, which feels a little like a jerky roller-coaster ride in the original Greek, and the somewhat cumbersome narrative of Matthew, which is regularly interrupted by lengthy theological and ethical discourses. Luke is a Gospel that emphasizes the "here and now" with statements like "God's kingdom is in our midst!" It celebrates the idea of having fellowship at table, sharing food with friend and stranger alike. It is a Gospel that is expressly concerned with sharing the good news with the whole Gentile world. This last concern may be the most persuasive message of the whole text: all are welcome.

For Luke, I longed to draw a house that conjured those same positive emotions: the smell of delicious food being prepared, the sound of children playing, and the warmth of family gathered together. I thought the house should showcase an environment where being in the moment, the "here and now," could be the focal experiential reality of all who enter. I have happy memories of visiting my grandparent's farm in rural Kentucky as a child, and my favorite place there was the large covered porch. One could sit there for hours and watch the infrequent vehicles drive down the gravel road in front of the house. Everyone waved as they passed by; a few stopped to investigate the identity of the visitors. Everyone was welcome, as there were no strangers out in the country. If you sat on the porch for long, you could meet and talk with every friend and family member who lived within ten miles of the farm as they passed through. The pace of life there was so much slower than at my home in the city. In many ways, the people were so much friendlier. The food always seemed to taste better there too. The cucumbers and tomatoes were fresher. When baked pies or fresh biscuits were removed from the oven, the aroma would drift out of the kitchen and people would gather to share time around the table.

This house invites me in to be with, or to become, family. That seems to be Luke's primary theme. For Luke, Jesus came to bring the kingdom of God to all people, meeting them where they are. It is a perspective that recognizes how God's family needs to grow beyond one tribe or nation to better align with God's vision of family. All people must be made to feel welcome and loved.

ARTIST'S REFLECTIONS
ON JOHN'S HOUSE

JOHN'S NARRATIVE STANDS IN STARK CONTRAST TO the traditional narratives of the Synoptic Gospels. Packed with theological constructs and symbolic gestures, it endeavors to shine a great light into the darkness around it—and the darkness cannot overcome it. This Gospel's depiction of Jesus contrasts with the Synoptics in significant ways. In the Synoptic tradition, Jesus responds to a request for a sign of his divinity by saying that no signs shall be given to this wicked generation. Mark has Jesus frequently warning those who witness his miracles to not tell anyone what they have seen. John takes the opposite approach, presenting Jesus' miracles less as acts of kindness and more as deliberate signs of who Jesus is: divinity incarnate. The author of John even writes repeatedly that these signs have been written down so that all may believe. John is a Gospel that seeks to avoid subtlety in blatantly spotlighting the Christ. There are no shepherds or angels in this story. John doesn't care about birth stories; he starts by telling us that Jesus was with God "in the beginning." Jesus has always been part of the divine plan to redeem creation even as the first light was spoken into being by the very word of God.

I thought John's house needed to reflect the boldness of John's Gospel, and it also needed to contrast with the more traditional houses of the other Gospels. I envisioned a very modern house with lots of glass and a geometry that emphasizes its juxtaposition against its wooded context. I pictured a night scene. The observer is advancing through the darkness. There are woods in every direction. And then the house appears as a brilliant source of light that illumines the path and surroundings. Once the house has been seen, the observer can't turn away from it. Instead, one is drawn in and invited to explore its surprises and mysteries. It is like walking inside a complex work of art. Around every corner are new vistas and geometric patterns that inspire one's mind to contemplate the potential meaning of the symbolic architectural gestures, just as the Gospel of John invites the reader to ponder the double and triple meanings of its carefully chosen words. The most compelling aspect of the house is the way the geometric windows and transparent layers inside transmit light into the dark surroundings. There is a bright source of warmth, emanating from the center of this modern structure, that cannot be extinguished. Every surface that the light falls on is warmed, even the snow. Once you're inside, a sense of intellectual contentment takes hold. There are a lifetime of philosophical mysteries in this place, and just like the Gospel of John, they invite a lifetime of study and consideration. This house is not just a new combination of the traditional elements of the house; it presents a bold new way of expressing the essence of home. Similarly, the Gospel of John is not so much another story about a man who is trying to teach us what God is about; it is a Gospel that presents a man who actually *is* the essence of God.

Prayers and Questions
for Reflection

WEEK 1

Christmas at Mark's House

OPENING PRAYER

Once more, Eternal God, we hope to experience the astonishing and radical mystery of the incarnation of your Son. Draw us into a place of silence and wonder amid the frantic whirl of the season. Make us aware of your presence as we seek a deeper understanding of the gift of your Son, Jesus Christ. Amen.

QUESTIONS FOR REFLECTION

1. How do you decorate for Christmas in your home? How do your decorations indicate what you cherish? How do they reflect your family's personality?

2. How does the author explain the lack of a Christmas narrative in Mark?

3. What is meant by the following: Mark could be called "a passion narrative with a long introduction"?

4. Why does Mark leave Christmas narratives on the cutting-room floor?

5. What do you think of the artist's depiction of Mark's house? If you were creating a picture of Mark's house, what, if anything, would you do differently? Why?

6. What issues in our present political or social context are causing you anxiety in this season? What leads you to feel despair or discouragement?

7. The author tells us that hope is to be found in the manger only because it is found first on the cross. What, in this season, is a source of hope for you?

CLOSING PRAYER

God of grace, we give thanks for the gift of your Son. By your Spirit, grant us the sure knowledge that we need not fear the grave, for Christ was born to save! As we begin the Advent journey, make us ever more aware that our hope is not in the cradle but in the cross. In the name of Jesus Christ we pray. Amen.

WEEK 2

Christmas at Matthew's House

OPENING PRAYER

In the midst of the accelerating frenzy of the holiday shopping season, O God, we yearn for a more compelling sense of your presence. Draw us into a quiet space where we may encounter your Son, Immanuel—"God with us." Amen.

QUESTIONS FOR REFLECTION

1. Read Matthew 1:1. For comparison, read Mark 1:1. What does each of these Gospel accounts say about how the good news begins?

2. What titles does each Gospel writer ascribe to Jesus, and what does that communicate about Jesus and about what the writer will emphasize in his story?

3. What does the inclusion of the women in Matthew's genealogy point to? What might we infer Matthew is trying to communicate by including them?

4. Read Matthew 2:1–12. Based on this text and the information in the chapter, what is different about the description of these visitors from how they have been typically described?

5. Consider each of the women named in Matthew's genealogy and the magi. Identify and jot down aspects of each of them that mark them as outsiders.

6. The author writes:

> God's vision encompasses both those to whom God has revealed Godself and the whole world and all who are made in God's image. God's promise is indeed for those of us who find our heart's true home in Jesus Christ. But it is also for the whole world that God loves so much.

- What do you think this statement has to say to us about the inclusion of brothers and sisters of other faiths in God's promises? Do you think it is necessary for persons to be Christian to be a part of Matthew's family picture gallery?

- How would you interpret these words to apply to the rest of the human family? How do you imagine it might impact the way we live in the created world?

7. Consider who in our contemporary context might be identified as outsiders—persons in your own family or among those with whom you interact who are not included for some reason, plus persons or groups presently being singled out by our society as not belonging. What do you think is the implication for those persons or groups that the good news is for all people—the whole of human society?

CLOSING PRAYER

We give thanks, O God, for the gift of Jesus Christ, your enduring presence with us. Guide us as we continue to discern what it means that the promise is for us—for the great big *us*—the whole human community. Open our hearts to a clearer understanding of your vision for the cosmos. For it is in the name of Immanuel we pray. Amen.

WEEK 3

Christmas at Luke's House

OPENING PRAYER

Holy God, as the candles' warmth envelops us, we are drawn to the sense of comfort and peace we find in Luke's beloved story. Guide us as we seek to enter more deeply into this account. Sharpen our awareness and open our hearts to what you would reveal. In the name of the Messiah we pray. Amen.

QUESTIONS FOR REFLECTION

1. Why would we not find the magi among Luke's lawn decorations?

2. What messages are communicated when lawn decorations mix manger scenes and blow-up Santas with sleighs? Would you say such decorations are in sync with Luke's themes or not? Why?

3. What does the author mean when she tells us that the first three chapters of Luke are like videos, each of which has a time/date stamp on it?

4. We read that the angels' heavenly music is not just a pious sentiment. What meaning does Luke intend to convey by including song?

5. Caesar Augustus styled himself as lord and savior of the world over which he ruled, and worshiping the emperor was part of the fabric of the culture. In our own time, can you identify persons, groups, or prevailing systems that seem to compete with Jesus Christ for our allegiance? If so, where do you see evidence of this in the current holiday season?

6. For Luke, where does the good news begin?

7. When you look at the world in which we are living now, what do you see with your eyes?

8. When you look at the world with the eyes of faith, where do you see glimpses of God's promises?

9. In response to the realities of the wounds of the world, how will you shape a faithful response?

CLOSING PRAYER

Eternal and loving God, we have heard good news! Despite what we can observe about our present world, you have not forgotten your world or those most in need of healing. In this season, help us to act on your good news of great joy, that your realm may be more real for all creation. Amen.

WEEK 4

Christmas at John's House and One Last Stop

OPENING PRAYER

Creator God, guide us as we seek to better discern the profound mystery of incarnation. It is with awe and wonder that we affirm this mystery we can never fully comprehend. Guide us as together we seek to explore more deeply the gift of the word made flesh. Amen.

QUESTIONS FOR REFLECTION

1. The author tells us that John's house is like none of the other three. In what ways is it unique?

2. We are told that for the other three Gospel writers, the good news begins at some point in human history, but John has another response. According to John, what was at the beginning with God?

3. If God has moved into the neighborhood—any neighborhood, all neighborhoods—what does God experience of the human condition? What do you imagine God calls us to do as a result of our own ongoing transformations?

4. For us, as deeply flawed human beings, what about the incarnation can be the source of our hope?

5. How is Isaiah a "spiritual grandparent" to the four Gospels?

6. Who were your spiritual grandparents, and how did they shape your values?

7. What hope are you passing on to others this season?

8. What commitment might you make this coming year to shed light on the world?

CLOSING PRAYER

Though no one has ever seen you, O God, we respond with wonder and awe to the good news that your Son, who is close to your heart, has made you known to us. As we draw near to the time when we celebrate the coming of your Son into the world, make us ever more aware that the Word has been made flesh and dwells among us. Amen.

Ideas for Study Groups

IDEAS FOR
STUDY GROUPS

After a time of greeting and introducing visitors, begin each meeting with the suggested opening prayer and enter a time of discussing some or all the reflection questions provided. Consider incorporating some of the following ideas into your time as well.

– Set up four candles for a candle lighting and have matches or a lighter available.

Alternatively, use electronic candles. It is not necessary that the candles be in an Advent wreath. As you begin each week, invite participants to sit in silence for a few moments. Then call their attention to the object you place in front of each week's candle and follow the directions below. After the first week, for each session that follows, read the phrases of earlier weeks as you light the candles, ending with the current week's candle lighting.

– **Week One:** a simple cross. Say, "From Mark's perspective, the cross, not the cradle, is the key symbol for the entire Gospel house." Light the candle with the words, "Come, Jesus Christ, Son of God." Pray the opening prayer.

– **Week Two:** a small family picture. Say, "In Matthew's house, our attention is drawn back to the generations preceding Jesus' birth." Light the candle with the words, "Come, Immanuel." Pray the opening prayer.

– **Week Three:** a manger. Say, "Luke is the Gospel that gives us the Christmas we know best, a place of warmth and safety, despite there being no room in the inn." Light the candle with the words, "Come, our Savior, Christ the Lord." Pray the opening prayer.

– **Week Four:** picture of Earth. Say, "In John's house, our attention is drawn back to the very beginning of creation." Light the candle with the words, "Jesus Christ, light of the world, Word made flesh." Pray the opening prayer.

– Each week before the session begins, post a piece of newsprint and title it with that week's Gospel house. Down the left margin of the sheet, print the following four categories: Christmas story?; Main message/key concepts; Symbol; House interior. Using that week's chapter and artist's description, fill in the categories as a group. As you add a Gospel each week, compare and contrast previous themes with the current Gospel's themes.

– Sing a hymn each week with the themes of the Gospel and discuss it. Following are some suggestions:

– **Week One:** "Good Christian Friends, Rejoice"

- **Week Two:** "Joy to the World"
- **Week Three:** "Angels We Have Heard on High," "Hark, the Herald Angels Sing," or "Go Tell It on the Mountain"
- **Week Four:** "O Come, O Come, Emmanuel"
- Consider projecting the illustration of the Gospel house being discussed each week.